THE GREAT OUTDOORS
KAYAKING AND RAFTING

By Raymond Harasymiw

Gareth Stevens
Publishing

Please visit our website, www.garethstevens.com. For a free color catalog of all our high-quality books, call toll free 1-800-542-2595 or fax 1-877-542-2596.

Library of Congress Cataloging-in-Publication Data

Harasymiw, Raymond.
Kayaking and rafting / Raymond Harasymiw.
    p. cm. — (The great outdoors)
Includes index.
ISBN 978-1-4339-7104-4 (pbk.)
ISBN 978-1-4339-7105-1 (6-pack)
ISBN 978-1-4339-7103-7 (library binding)
1. Kayaking. 2. Rafting (Sports) I. Title.
GV783.H35 2012
797.1—dc23

2011051419

First Edition

Published in 2013 by
Gareth Stevens Publishing
111 East 14th Street, Suite 349
New York, NY 10003

Copyright © 2013 Gareth Stevens Publishing

Designer: Michael J. Flynn
Editor: Therese Shea

Photo credits: Cover, p. 1 ©iStockphoto.com/kali9; p. 5 (left) Pecold/Shutterstock.com; p. 5 (right) ©iStockphoto.com/slobo; pp. 6, 13 ©iStockphoto.com/Joe Michl; p. 9 (main) Lifesize/Thomas Northcut/Getty Images; p. 9 (inset) ©iStockphoto.com/Evgenia Fashayan; p. 10 ©iStockphoto.com/Sylvia Schug; p. 15 Aurora/Jack Montgomery/Getty Images; p. 17 VILevi/Shutterstock.com; p. 21 Jonathan Noden-Wilkinson/Shutterstock.com.

Printed in the United States of America

CPSIA compliance information: Batch #CS12GS: For further information contact Gareth Stevens, New York, New York at 1-800-542-2595.

CONTENTS

DEC 8 2012

Words in the glossary appear in **bold** type the first time they are used in the text.

GET READY TO PADDLE!

Do you like boats and being on water? Do you want to be the captain of your own boat? Kayaking and rafting offer hands-on adventure, exercise, and fun for all ages.

A day in a kayak or raft can be relaxing—or it can be wet and wild! Beginners should start out in calm waters. After they gain more **experience**, they can "shoot the **rapids**." It's time to put on your life jacket and learn more about these water sports!

4

Both life jackets and **helmets** are important for rafting and kayaking.

rafting   kayaking

5

"White water" is a name for fast-flowing water, like the river this kayaker is in.

ALL KINDS OF KAYAKING

A kayak is a small, lightweight boat. Kayakers face forward and move the boat with a paddle that has a blade on each side.

Kayaks have different shapes to match different kinds of kayaking. **Recreational** kayakers use touring or sea kayaks. These flat-bottomed boats allow people to paddle the calm waters of a lake, ocean shore, or river. Whitewater kayaks have rounded bottoms and are best to carry people through rough river rapids. Other kayaks are shaped somewhat like a surfboard and are used to surf ocean waves.

INTO THE WILD

Native peoples in the far north were the first to use kayaks – more than 6,000 years ago! They made them from wood and animal skins.

ALL KINDS OF KAYAKS

When most people think of kayaks, they think of **rigid** boats. Some rigid kayaks are plastic. Plastic, though inexpensive, can be heavy to carry in and out of the water. **Fiberglass** is a lighter but pricier choice. Kayaks can be as light as 20 pounds (9 kg) or heavier than 80 pounds (36 kg). Folding and inflatable kayaks are easier to carry and store than rigid kayaks. **Inflatable** kayaks are popular with beginners because of their low price. However, they're harder to control than rigid kayaks.

INTO THE WILD

Kayak racing has been featured in the **Olympics** since 1936.

8

Multiseat kayaks are great for pairing experienced paddlers and beginners.

inflatable kayaks

9

Paddles come in different lengths and different weights, just like the kayaks themselves.

PADDLES AND STROKES

There are different kinds of paddles. Wider blades allow for great speed, but they require more force to pull them. Narrow blades mean more strokes, but less effort. Kayakers use both their arms and back, so neither gets too tired.

The forward stroke begins with the tip of the blade near the kayaker's ankles. The kayaker pulls the blade back toward the hip and lifts it from the water. The motion is repeated on the other side. Special strokes move the kayak backward and sideways. Sweep strokes turn it around.

INTO THE WILD

Racing kayakers use short paddles so they can row faster.

11

DON'T TIP!

Beginners want their kayaks to feel **stable**. However, a kayak that feels unstable at first is often more stable in big waves. In addition, the more stable a boat feels, the slower it travels through the water.

The shape of a kayak is important, too. A wider kayak is more stable than a narrow kayak, but it's slower. A shorter kayak, such as a whitewater kayak, is easier to turn than a longer kayak. However, a longer kayak is easier to paddle in a straight line.

INTO THE WILD

A kayak may cost from $100 to several thousand dollars!

A kayak that seems "tippy" at first will be more forgiving in waves, leaning instead of tipping over.

LET'S ROLL

Whitewater kayaks have tight **cockpits**. Kayakers in these boats need to learn how to "roll" in case their boat overturns, or capsizes. Rolling helps them turn the kayak right side up without getting out of the cockpit. Whitewater kayakers also wear "spray skirts" around their waist. These fit over the cockpit opening and keep water out of the boat when rolling and in rough conditions.

Some sea kayaks are made to let paddlers sit on top. These boats are good for those nervous about rolling or climbing out of a capsized kayak.

HOW TO ROLL A KAYAK

1. While upside down, place your body forward against the front of the kayak.

2. With both hands, place your paddle **parallel** to one side of the kayak, reaching out of the water.

3. Move your paddle so that one blade is out of the water, resting against the boat, and **perpendicular** to the boat.

4. Rest your head against the shoulder closest to the blade above the water.

5. Snap your hips to move the boat to the upright position.

ALL TOGETHER NOW

While people can kayak alone, rafting usually requires a group of people. Most paddle rafts are inflatable, rectangular, and hold four to eight people. Rafting a river can be peaceful, allowing people to float easily along. Or it can be a fast-paced, wet, whitewater adventure!

Some rafts have motors, but most people like paddling themselves. Rafters usually work as a team. Each side paddles to move the boat. Some people raft for several days and camp at night.

Whitewater rafts are usually 12 to 16 feet (3.7 to 4.9 m) long. However, some are smaller and hold just one or two people.

17

RATING THE RAPIDS

River rapids range from bumpy to fall-out-of-the-raft conditions. Rivers are rated using **roman numerals** to let rafters know what they'll experience. As the numbers go up, the danger increases. Check out the rating system on the opposite page.

Inexperienced rafters who want to travel down rivers with class III rapids or higher should check with local whitewater rafting businesses. These companies provide rafts, gear, and a guide to get groups safely down the river.

THE INTERNATIONAL SCALE OF RIVER DIFFICULTY

Class I:
Easy. Fast-moving water with small waves. No rocks. Guide not needed.

Class II:
Medium. Some rapids but clear path. Guide not needed.

Class III:
Moderate. Many strong waves. Rocks. Some experience needed. Guide helpful.

Class IV:
Difficult. Long, powerful rapids requiring experienced boat handling. Guide needed.

Class V:
Extremely difficult. Long, violent rapids. Steep drops. Many rocks. Only experienced rafters with a guide.

Class VI:
Unrunnable. Don't even think about it!

SAFE PADDLING!

As fun as rafting looks, safety is always a concern. Rafters should wear both helmets and life jackets. Many rivers have rocks, logs, and other objects in their path. It's important to know how to direct the raft around these dangers to keep both the raft and the people in it safe. That's why a guide is important on rivers with rapids.

If you're ready to have fun and maybe get a bit wet, kayaking and rafting are the water sports for you! Get paddling!

INTO THE WILD

People with lots of whitewater rafting experience are called "river rats."

Though the raft is large and inflatable, rafters can easily get thrown out of the raft in whitewater rapids.

21

GLOSSARY

cockpit: the space where a person sits inside a kayak

experience: knowledge and skill gained by doing something many times

fiberglass: glass fibers pressed into a hard material. Used in making various products.

helmet: a hard hat or other head covering to guard the head from harm

inflatable: able to be filled with gas or air

Olympics: a sporting event held every 4 years in which many countries take part

parallel: describing lines or objects that are the same distance apart at all points

perpendicular: describing two lines or objects that cross to form right, or 90°, angles

rapids: a fast-moving part of a river with rocks and other objects in it

recreational: describing activities done to have fun

rigid: unbending

roman numeral: any of the letters used by the ancient Romans to stand for numbers, including I for 1, V for 5, and X for 10

stable: steady and not likely to move

FOR MORE INFORMATION

BOOKS

Bodden, Valerie. *Kayaking.* Mankato, MN: Creative Education, 2009.

Mason, Paul. *Kayaking and Rafting.* North Mankato, MN: Smart Apple Media, 2008.

McFee, Shane. *Whitewater Rafting.* New York, NY: Rosen Publishing Group, 2008.

WEBSITES

How Whitewater Rafting Works
www.howstuffworks.com/outdoor-activities/water-sports/white-water-rafting.htm
Learn more about the excitement of riding the rapids.

Learn to Eskimo Roll Your Kayak
paddling.about.com/od/technique/tp/Eskimo_Roll_Kayak.htm
Read more about rolling a kayak, sometimes called Eskimo rolling,
and see photos of how it's done.

INDEX